茗榮兄

雅正

填敏

2021.

See/Sea Mandala

王慎敏 Simon Wang

海的曼荼羅

長歌藝術傳播負責人、長歌出版社社長／吳　放

海，存在不枯不竭的恆定狀態，又兼有不止不息的潮汐變化。如此趨近永恆，又如此流變無常，多麼像是人生！海，具有安定人心的自然力量，人間種種事物相對於海，都顯得微不足道。在文明社會物質生活中所積累的憂慮煩擾，往往在海邊瞭望時可以獲得紓解。看海，向來是療癒心神的良方。

王慎敏先生近年來頻頻去看海，也不停地畫畫，大批畫作盡是海景，包括海岸石礫。水與石的本質樣貌大致如一，而動態位置則變化多端。我初次在他畫室裡，乍見這些巨幅海水、眾多卵石，一時因廣袤、繁密的景物感到震懾，然後又因單純、遼闊的畫面，覺得平靜、悠遠。問他為何畫海？只聽他回應：「這畫的是曼荼羅。」我立刻懂得了這位畫家，以及他的畫。

曼荼羅，蘊含佛教宇宙觀，是一種幻想的宇宙圖，信眾藉以作為心靈觀想對象，來修習教義。慎敏兄援引「曼荼羅」的意涵，來表達面對大海的感受，以及執筆畫圖的心境。每天潛心作畫十多小時，如同閉關修行；畫完一幅又一幅相同題材，可比僧侶繪製沙畫，透過周而復始的創作過程，去體認當下的存在，與永恆的虛幻。把這一系列關於海的繪畫，以「曼荼羅」為名，足可理解他將藝術創作的外相表現，對照內心思維，欲從外觀瞭望中看清自然，也往內觀省視中認識自我。

慎敏兄曾追隨冉茂芹老師習畫，畫過無數靜物和人像。他深刻記憶老師的教導——「目中無物，心觀其理」，觀看世界不能受限於物體表相，要用心觀想其內在道理。於是他總想著以繪畫來「弘道」，彰顯藝術的精神性。後來他自己畫海，將海邊的磊磊石頭，想像成芸芸眾生，用畫人頭的心思技法去畫石頭，曾自作一詩：「人頭石頭都是頭，頭頭是道道是頭，道不能通石非頭，道通頭通石是頭。」如禪詩偈語一般，表達出畫面背後的隱喻。他是藉由畫海水、畫石頭，來體現具有雋永意義而難以言說之道理。

雖然使用西方的油畫顏料，慎敏兄別能描繪出東方山水的意境，兼有自然、人文之美，包含陰陽、動靜之理。我能從靜止的石頭上看到活潑的生命，在停駐的潮水中聽見湧動的心聲。在他的畫裡，一片海洋即是一片心靈，無數石頭象徵無數人群，其中有人與海的對話，主體生命與客觀世界的共鳴。我感知他畫中帶有濃濃詩意、深深哲理，這是其顯著的繪畫風格。他透過具象的自然景觀，傳達抽象的心靈思維，這正是東方藝術的特徵。

經由一個善緣引介，得與慎敏兄相識論交，並協助策辦畫展、編印畫冊，有幸親近他的傑作，因而重新發現海的美麗與意義。祝願慎敏兄持續在繪畫境界裡不斷提升精進，也盼望這一系列「海的曼荼羅」畫作，能為觀賞者提供更寬廣新穎的視野，可以放眼瞭望海天一色，也可以細細觀賞一粒石頭、一朵浪花，或一抹苔痕；可以深深思慮宇宙奧妙，也可以慢慢感通人生智慧，或什麼都不想，只讓心情靜靜地沉澱下來，也就夠了。

See/Sea Mandala

by Wu Fund, Founder of Chang Ge Arts & Media

The sea encompasses a boundless, perpetual state, endlessly changing with the tides. Almost eternal, and yet volatile too, like life! The sea has an inherent power to soothe, while all things in the corporal world are trivial in the face of the sea. Our amassed troubles and distractions from the material world are alleviated when looking at the sea. Watching the sea is a good way to heal the mind.

In recent years, Mr. Simon Wang frequents the sea, and has been painting ceaselessly. Many of his paintings are of seascapes, including beach rocks. The essence of water and stone is more or less the same, but the dynamic positions vary greatly. When I was in his studio for the first time, I saw immense expanses of seawater and numerous pebbles. For a while, I was astounded by the broad and dense scenery, and also calm and remote because of its simple and vast imagery. When I asked him why he paints the sea, his only response was, "I'm painting Mandala." I immediately understood the painter and his paintings.

The mandala embodies Tibetan Buddhist cosmology as a fantastic cosmic map, while believers use the mandala as an object of spiritual visualization to practice meditation. Simon cites the meaning of "mandala" to convey his sentiments of facing the sea and his state of mind when painting. Painting for more than ten hours a day is a retreat; painting the same subject in one painting after another is comparable to monks making sand mandala. Through repeated creative process, one experiences the existence of the present and eternal illusion. Titling this series of paintings of the sea under the name of "mandala" is sufficient in comprehending the artist's expression of artistic creation, complementing his thoughts and desire to understand nature, and to know oneself through introspection.

Simon once painted countless still lifes and portraits during his studies with Mr. Yim Maukun. He keenly recalls his teacher's teaching, "nothing is seen, but the mind knows the truth." When perceiving the world, one cannot be bound by appearance, the inner truth must be seen with the mind. Simon strives to wield painting to "promote the way," and underscore the spirituality of art. Later he would paint the sea, seeing stones as sentient beings, applying methods of painting portraits to painting stones, and write the poem: "Portraits and stones are semblances. Semblances all lead to the way; if the way is obscure, then truth is unclear. When the way is clear, portraits and stones all point to truth." Like a Zen poem or Buddhist chant, expressing a metaphor behind the image. Simon utilizes paintings of seawater and stone to encapsulate the persistent, indescribable truth.

Though working with Western oil paints, Simon still depicts an air of Eastern *shanshui* landscapes, with the beauty of nature and the arts, which include principles of yin and yang, movement and stillness. I sense spirit in still rocks, and a surging heartbeat in stagnant tides. In his paintings, the ocean is a piece of mind, countless stones symbolize countless beings, among them some people converse with the sea, and subjective life resonates with the objective world. I perceive the deeply poetic and philosophical aspects of his paintings, which is notably his own style. He conveys abstract, rational thinking through tangible, natural landscape, which is characteristic of Eastern Art.

Through the introduction of a mutual friend, I met Simon and assisted him in the planning and compilation of his exhibition and catalogue. I feel most honored to be able to familiarize myself with his masterpieces, and rediscover the beauty and meaning of the sea. I wish Simon continuous progress in the realm of painting, and I hope this series of "See/Sea Mandala" may provide viewers with a broader and imaginative perspective. You can look out onto the sea and the sky, or regard each stone, each wave or every trace of moss. You can contemplate the mystery of the universe or consider the insight of life, or nothing at all. Still the mind, and that is enough.

自序

噢耶！終於要辦第一次個人畫展了，畫了超過 60 年，也不知道自己在畫什麼。
即將到來的畫展是多年畫畫的果，但什麼是我畫畫的因？

01 ╱ 年少心懷丹青志　哪知汲汲營生苦
　　　　峰迴路轉情更熾　緣在志在藝不衰

我很小就愛畫畫，父母也很以此為榮，小學時，每個星期日父親必定送我去馬白水老師那裡學畫水彩，到了五年級，畫畫就被升學壓力淹沒了，初中、高中時期，只有在美術比賽時，老師才會偶然想到我，我也才短暫意識到我還有這項才能。但到了要考大學時，我要考美術系就成了身在企業界父親不可接受的難題，我只好退而求其次選擇建築系，但擦身考上土木系，準備念一年再轉建築系。一年間幾經父子懇談，我還是當了「好兒子」轉念工業工程，至少與企管系滿接近的。

大學畢業、服役當兵、出國念書，是當時台灣青年的指標模式。我在美國德州念完碩士，在加州灣區矽谷找到工作，結了婚，買了房子，每天朝九晚五，週末聚餐烤肉，生活穩定到讓人害怕。此時台灣又來了召集令，父親要我回台灣幫他的忙，想想，人生如棋子走一步算一步，反正美國文化也不適合我。

回台灣在工廠做過工程師，也做過企劃，還當過行銷部主管，自認表現差強。工作之餘我以攝影取代畫畫來填補藝術的空虛，也有緣認識一些登山好友，開啟我山岳攝影之途。1993 年，家族投資發生變化，我的財務壓力大增，在所有親朋好友萬般不解下辭掉了工作，不到 40 歲就退休，從此與賢妻靠投資股票為生，真要由衷感謝賢妻與眾多好友相互扶持，關關難過關關過，能幸福活到現在。更幸福的是有機會在家當「奶爸」，和兒子一起打球、溜冰、爬山、玩樂高、打爵士鼓，想想多少人能有第二次童年？

02 ╱ 攝影當畫剎那成　飄然曠野自在景
　　　　黃山心境即我心　世界之巔生死悟

在此同時我也開始我 10 年《見山》計劃，以減肥、跑步、舉重健身為開端，到「視丘攝影」向吳嘉寶老師學習 4×5 大型相機商業攝影，再向黃昭雄老師學習山水國畫，1996 年在「恆昶藝廊」舉辦《飄然曠野》攝影個展，展出我以 4×5 相機所攝，放大至 40 吋 ×50 吋，以美國壯闊山野為主題的攝影作品。

1994 年開始，已經在黃山展開我下一個階段的拍攝。黃山在中國美術史上至為重要，但黃山能拍的就是那麼幾個點，想拍出新意很困難，只能靠時間和體力了。四年期間上山十多次，曾經最長在山上住過兩個月，每天和當地朋友胡為民帶著繩索，下深谷上險峰尋找新的拍攝點，慢慢走、耐心等、細細拍。1998 年在深圳出版《黃山心境》攝影專輯，是至今少數以 4×5 大型相機表現黃山的攝影專輯之一。

1996 年四月，第一次登上海拔 5545 公尺的卡拉帕塔（Kala Patthar peak），看見世界第一高峰——聖母峰，之後八年，陸續在尼泊爾、錫金、西藏、巴基斯坦拍攝超過 8000 公尺的 14 座高峰，數次與死神擦身，是生與死面對面的體會，2003 年完成《世界之巔》拍攝。之後繼續在中國大陸拍攝高山，2005 年完成《自在神州》，是否見山悟道不得而知，拍到的影像似乎也不重要，所有底拍至今仍敝帚自珍般地深鎖在乾燥櫃中從未面世。

03

師道藝道起善緣　彩筆孜孜意不倦
目中無物心觀理　勝解方知取捨難

2000 年世紀交替，在喜瑪拉雅山冰雪封山的冬季，在朋友介紹下，至蘭陽畫室向楊德俊老師學習油畫和粉彩，楊老師是台灣專注在粉彩創作的先趨，在他的指導下和其他同學共同組織了「中華民國粉彩推廣協會」，2004 年又與熱心粉彩的梁玉燦會長及旅美畫友共同組建了「台北粉彩協會」。當時我以油畫當練習，粉彩靜物寫生當創作，經常參加國內外展覽與比賽，2007 年榮獲美國藝術家聯合會（The Allied Artists of America）公開賽 PSA 獎，縱使如此，仍深覺繪畫基礎不如科班同學扎實，但要回學校從頭學起又是困難重重。

去冉茂芹老師的雙橋畫室學畫是緣分，而且是註定的緣分，先是一位好友向我推薦，我還在猶豫時另一位好友又向我推薦，再隔兩天法國的粉彩畫友 Sylvie Cabal 來台灣，特地約了冉老師教她畫人像，要我去當翻譯，這是我與冉老師第一次見面，經過兩天的翻譯，我下定決心跟冉老師習畫，一學就是七年。

「師者，傳道、授業、解惑也」，一般畫畫老師都偏向技藝的傳授，很少有人志在宏「藝術之道」。冉老師在技藝部分講求習畫要扎實，所以在人體素描要求同學要明瞭與熟記人體結構的骨骼肌肉，並要求反覆練習。在藝道上要求「勝解」，勝解是不但要能夠理解，還要有決定取捨的能力，他常說「目中無物，心觀其理」，表面看起來是「物」，只看表面就會困於「物」，我們看到的是「相」，相是由「理」合聚而成，能觀其理才會有取捨的能力，這是我在冉老師那裡學習的最大收穫。

04

海景難解亦難畫　瞬間風雲千萬變
勤拍慎選細觀理　畫理自成海入畫

人生最難的莫過於斷、捨、離，離開冉老師也是如此，但又不得不如此，因為不離開就找不到自己。剛開始悶在自己畫室畫些素描，胡亂畫些油畫，真是迷惘到毫無方向。有一天無意看到過去我拍的海景，就挑了一張來畫，畫起來還蠻有感覺的。

畫界很反對描繪相片，其實也沒錯，相片色彩的層次與寫生現況相差太大，況且還有投機取巧之嫌。還好我之前在海邊畫過很多寫生，稍能「勝解」海邊的狀況，畫出來不會太像相片。試了幾幅，我開始思考以海為主題畫一系列海景，因為太沉醉於浪濤之中。

海景很難畫，因為變化太快，要畫大幅的海景更是困難，畫自己拍的攝影變成唯一的選擇。畫海沒有攝影還真辦不了事，人的視覺暫留是 1/16 秒，人天生就是沒辦法把海浪在視覺上暫留成一個形。在攝影發明之前，前輩畫家對海浪的描繪千奇百怪，最知名的大概就是葛飾北齋〈神奈川沖浪裡〉的龍爪浪了，但現在我如果還是像葛飾北齋那樣畫也會怪怪的。現在還有高速閃光攝影，可以拍出子彈貫穿蘋果的瞬間，這些都是輔助人類天生的不足，讓我們能「眼觀其理」。透過相片，我可以看得到更多細部的變化，看多了，「眼觀其理」慢慢就串成「心觀其理」，那就離「勝解」不遠矣。

捨棄過去拍的海景不用，選擇重新開始也是必然的，擇地、擇時、擇潮拍攝我要畫的海景，尤其是海浪最難掌控，浪形位置不對，整體構圖就不對，常要拍數十張才有一張滿意的。以前去海邊寫生，去到哪兒有什麼畫什麼，比較不會去講究潮汐、浪形、晨昏、季節的變化。重新出發後，常為了潮汐（低潮時石頭前景才多）、日出，清晨三點起床，三點半出門，五點開拍。冬末初春趕著拍綠色的海苔，炎炎夏日趕著拍退去青苔、裸露原色的石頭。

05 理性平衡是構圖　色彩清心即印象
　　　　筆觸如皴意隨興　海景心景自在心

攝影與繪畫有很多相似之處，要重新出發總該有一些思想準備吧！要有怎樣的構圖？要有怎樣的筆觸？還要有怎樣的色彩？

攝影作品的好壞構圖舉足輕重，過去的攝影經驗與過程，我已鍛煉出自己特有構圖的風格。中國構圖思想比西方早，12 世紀南宋就有「馬一角、夏半邊」的構圖思維；西方構圖思維在文藝復興時興起，以理性思維講求構圖的理性視覺平衡。我以攝影基礎為經，文藝復興理性平衡為緯，成為我構圖的思想。

再來就是筆觸了，筆觸有如簽名，是最個人化的部分，油畫講究色塊，這也是我最缺乏學習的部分。以前隨黃昭雄老師畫過一段時間的山水國畫，如果以皴法來代替色塊可能嗎？要從頭練書法再練皴法嗎？考慮再三，啊！隨興吧！誰會在乎野和尚念經是否規規矩矩，浪漫隨興就成為我筆觸的思想。

顏色怎麼玩？又是一個難題，先畫吧！摸著石頭過河，船到橋頭自然直。畫了約兩個月，一天突發奇想，學印象派畫家丟掉黑色如何？原本攝影就沒黑色，況且我還蠻喜歡印象派的色調，試了一幅，覺得還真是我想要的，至此就與黑色說拜拜，色彩思想也定調了。

06 朝八晚六筆筆畫　如鼓如磬聲聲靜
　　　　巴哈音韻伴彩筆　日日精進逐浪花

就這樣畫著畫著畫了三年，每週五天，每天 8:00 畫到 18:00，有如閉關，和過去的畫友也少有來往。其實很多冉老師雙橋畫室的同學，也有和我一樣的困擾，是否要離開老師？如何才能找到自己？一天冉師畫室同窗名能兄來訪，見我海邊的石頭畫得還不錯，問我怎麼畫的，隔日我寫了一首打油詩給他：「人頭石頭都是頭，頭頭是道道是頭，道不能通石非頭，道通頭通石是頭。」我只是在說冉老師最擅長的就是人像畫，冉老師透過畫人頭來講述他的藝道，如果只看到頭而不見其道則道不能通，如果能見其道，畫石頭和畫人頭是一樣的道理，我只是用冉老師畫人頭的方法畫石頭罷了。

畫畫時聽音樂是必要的，音符像另一支無形的畫筆，潛移默化影響著畫面的造形與顏色。原本我就愛聽貝多芬，聽著畫著總覺得不搭，再試布拉姆斯，也不搭，蕭邦、馬勒、柴可夫斯基……都不搭，一天無意在網路上看到巴哈全套 144 張 CD，巴哈以前比較少聽，但似乎也沒怎麼猶豫就買了回來，一聽，啊！太搭了，巴洛克時代的音樂，變化中帶著規律像極了海浪，尤其是巴哈的宗教清唱劇，是他對上帝虔誠的心，更是人與天的對話。

07 　／ 百里迷霧千日畫　原是唐卡曼荼羅
　　　　　海景畫景心中鏡　無海無景心乃真

某日室內設計師好友雅文來我畫室，一看我的畫就說：「Simon！你是在畫唐卡。」想想也對，以前去尼泊爾、西藏，看過唐卡師父畫唐卡，不急不徐一筆一筆慢慢畫，一張唐卡有時候要一年才能完成，我畫畫過程是有些像在畫唐卡。無獨有偶，兩星期後法國粉彩畫家 Sylvie Cabal 來我畫室，一看我的畫就說：「你在畫曼荼羅（Mandala），我現在也在畫曼荼羅，只是形式不同。」她以前以畫花成名，整張紙只畫一朵花，層層花瓣有如幾何抽象；她立刻拿出新作品的相片給我看，花瓣已進化成曼荼羅圖案，造型顏色看起來非常療癒。她告訴我，她現在每天畫畫感覺被正能量圍繞著，都不會感到疲累，而且很快樂；這點倒和我的感覺非常相似，不但不累而且心靜自在又歡喜。當真我是在畫唐卡嗎？當真是在畫曼荼羅嗎？

唐卡，是西藏畫在布、絹或紙上的一種畫像，題材廣泛，有佛本尊像、金剛護法神像、祖師像等，幾乎包羅了西藏生活的所有內容。其中又以曼荼羅，又稱之為「壇城」最為重要，它是藏傳佛教整體宇宙觀的展現，由觀想曼荼羅進入自身內層的探索，以達到天與人相通相容的境界。千百年來眾多西藏高僧，以他自身所感悟的內心曼荼羅創作唐卡畫，希望能與觀畫者內心的曼荼羅對話。

其實每一個人內心都有屬於自己的曼荼羅，有的人正向且清晰，有的人負面而混亂，但它一直是我們人生價值觀的準繩。有時候面對一景或一物，由觀而想，由想生感，由感得悟，這就是外在的實景曼荼羅與我們內心的意像曼荼羅的對話。況且我們今世時時刻刻都會與過去世世代代對話，那就是在觀想 - 喚醒 - 面對 - 重整 - 改變中進行，人生的修行與轉變就在一念之間。

畫著畫著又畫了三年，思緒有如海、執著有如石，漸漸轉變成，思緒漸如石、執著漸如海，海的曼荼羅意象越發清晰。啊！是該與大家分享曼荼羅的時候了。

畫作完成就是一段緣的結束，又是另一段緣的開始，畫作要面對的不再是我，是更多藝術愛好者，畫作的曼荼羅是否能與觀賞者的曼荼羅對話？是緣分。無論有緣沒緣，有沒有曼荼羅？是不是曼荼羅？也已經不再重要，如能帶給觀者一絲法喜，那就足矣！

至於，什麼是我畫畫的因？年輕時想當畫家，謀生是因；中年隨興小作，抒發是因；至今潛心而畫，修行是因；因因相扣，就是冥冥中的隨緣吧！

Preface

by Simon Wang

Oh yeah! I am finally presenting my first solo exhibition of paintings. I have been painting for more than 60 years, and still I do not know what I paint. This upcoming exhibition is the result of many years of painting, but why do I paint?

01   *The young revere aspirations of art,*
how does one know the pain of making a living
Winding roads make for a more passionate mind
Fate is present, drive is there, art does not wane

From an early age, I have loved to paint, and this made my parents incredibly proud. During elementary school, my father would send me to Mr. Ma Paisui to study watercolor every Sunday, but academic pressure during fifth grade engulfed my classes. It was only during junior high and high school art competitions that my teachers would think of me, and I would realize for a short while that I still had the skills. When it came to the university entrance exams, it was unacceptable for me to major in art, seeing as my father worked in the corporate sector. I had to submit and choose architecture, but instead was admitted into civil engineering, intending to transfer to architecture after a year. After discussing many times with my father during this year, I deferred, deciding to be a "good son" and transferred to industrial engineering, which was at least similar to business management.

Graduating from university, serving military service, and studying abroad was one of the templates for Taiwanese youth at the time. I obtained my Master's Degree in Texas, got a job in the San Francisco Bay Area, got married, bought a house, and worked 9 to 5, barbecuing over the weekend, with an alarmingly anchored life. Then my father asked me to return to Taipei to help him with the family business, and I thought: life is like a game of chess, changing with each move. American culture was not for me anyway.

Back in Taiwan, I worked as a factory engineer, a planner and a marketing manager - I was quite good. Outside of work, I had replaced painting with photography to fill my art void, and got to know quite a few mountaineering friends, initiating my path into mountain photography. In 1993, the family business changed, and being under immense financial pressure, I quit my job against the vast confusion of family and friends, retiring before the age of 40. After that, I invested in stocks for a living with my wonderful wife. I want to thank my beloved wife and dear friends, who helped us during this difficult time, allowing us to live happily to the present. What is more enchanting than to be a "stay-at-home dad," playing ball, skating, hiking, playing Lego, and drumming with your son? How many people get a second childhood?

02 *Photography becomes painting in an instant*
Drifting in the wilderness
Huangshan mind and place is my mind
To know life and death at the peak of the world

During this time, I also began working on my decade-long project "Seeing the Mountain," with weight loss, running, weightlifting and fitness to start off. I attended the FOTOSOFT Institute of Photography to learn 4 x 5 large format commercial photography with Mr. Wu Jiabao, and Chinese *shanshui* landscape painting from Mr. Huang Chao-Hsiung. In 1996, I held the photography exhibition "Drifting in the Wilderness" at Fujifilm Taiwan Gallery, showcasing my 4 x 5 work, which was enlarged to 40 x 50 inches, showcasing the majestic mountains in the United States.

I started photographing Huangshan in 1994. Huangshan is very important in the history of Chinese art, but its perspectives are limited and difficult to shoot new views, which would require time and physical strength. Over the course of four years, I took more than 10 trips, the longest being 2 months in the mountains, bearing ropes with my local friend Hu Wei-Ming into the deep valleys and sharp ridges in search of new viewpoints, progressing slowly with patience and caution. The photographic album "Mt. Huangshan: Mind and Place" was published in Beijing in 1998, and is one of the few albums of Huangshan presented with a 4 x 5 large format field camera.

In April 1996, I ascended Kala Patthar Peak at the elevation of 5545 meters for the first time, and saw the world's highest peak—Mount Everest. In the following eight years, I continued to photograph 14 peaks over 8000 meters in Nepal, Sikkim, Tibet and Pakistan, brushing with death several times, and confronting my own mortality. In 2003, I finished the photographic album "The Peak of the World," followed by "Unbound in China" which documents the scenery in China. I am not sure if it is possible to know the way through mountains, and images are not important, so all my film is now locked up in dry cabinets like personal treasures.

03 *Serendipity in the way of teachers and art*
Brushes diligent and tireless
The mind sees truth when the eye sees not a thing,
knowing decision is Adhimoksha *complete understanding*

In 2000, at the change of the century, in the snowy winter of the Himalayas, a friend introduced me to Lan Yang Atelier to study oil painting and pastel with Mr. Yang Dejun. Mr. Yang is one of the pioneers of promoting pastel in Taiwan. We organized the "Pastel Art Promotion Association of Taiwan" with other students under his guidance, and in 2004 set up the "Pastel Association of Taiwan" with president Mr. Jack Liang and other overseas painters. At that time, I employed oil painting as practice and sketches, while still lifes in pastels were the artwork, often participating in domestic and international exhibitions and competitions. In 2007 I won the Allied Artists of America PSA award. However, even so, I still felt that my skills were not up to par with my classmates, and returning to school and beginning again would be difficult.

It was destined serendipity that I would learn painting at Mr. Yim Maukun's Shuangqiao studio. A friend first introduced the studio to me, and another while I was hesitating, and then two days later, my French pastel painter friend Sylvie Cabal was in Taiwan, and specifically requested Mr. Yim teach her to paint portraits, and asked me to accompany her as an interpreter. It was my first meeting with Mr. Yim, and after two days of translation, I decided that I wanted to learn from Mr. Yim, and that became 7 years.

"Teachers preach and teach by clearing confusion." Generally teachers teach skills, while very few are eager to teach "the way of art." Mr. Yim emphasized skill when it came to painting, so we were required to memorize and cover exercises in understanding the skeletal muscles of the body. In the path of art, we were asked to achieve "complete understanding," this solution was not just about understanding, but also having the ability to impart on the decision. Mr. Yim often said, "nothing is seen, but the mind knows the truth." On the surface we see "things," but when you only see "things," you become limited by "things," so we see "appearance" or "semblance," while semblance is composed of "reason." To understand its truth, you need the ability to make decisions. This is the most important thing I have learned from Mr. Yim.

04 *The seascape is difficult to resolve and paint,*
its state changes in an instant
With diligent shooting and careful selection, one sees the way of the sea
Knowing the way, sea flows into painting

The hardest thing in life is to part ways, surrender, or withdraw. Leaving Mr. Yim was the same, but it had to be, because you cannot find yourself without leaving. At the start, I drew sketches in the studio and painted oil paintings without much direction. One day, I saw photographs of seascapes that I shot, and picked one to paint - and it was quite interesting to paint. Painters are opposed to painting from photographs. And in fact it is quite true, the color and perspective in photography diverges from the actual situation in live sketches, and can feel like cheating. Fortunately, I had painted many sketches on the shore before, so I could "decide" on the state of the sea, and divert from photographs. After a few paintings, I began to consider a series of seascapes, because I was so immersed in the waves.

It is difficult to paint the sea because everything changes so quickly. It is even more demanding to paint large seascapes. Painting from my own photographs has become the only choice - It is almost impossible to paint the sea without photography.

Our visual persistence is but 1/16 seconds, and we are innately unable to grasp waves in a single form. Before the invention of photography, paintings of waves by our predecessors were strange. The most famous would probably be Katsushika Hokusai's *The Great Wave off Kanagawa*. But nowadays, it would be very odd to paint like Katsushika Hokusai. We now have high-speed photography, which can even capture the instant a bullet punctures an apple. This technology eases our innate shortcomings, and allows us to "see the truth." Through photography, I can see more detailed changes, and after seeing more, "seeing the truth" can slowly progress to "the mind seeing the truth," and that is not far from "complete understanding."

Renouncing seascapes of the past is inevitable for one to start again. I would choose a time, place and tide to shoot my preferred seascape, however, waves are the most difficult to control; if the form of the wave is in an unsuitable placement, the composition will feel wrong. Often one would have to take at least 10 photographs before one is satisfactory. Going to the shore to sketch, you draw whatever is there, and you are less likely to care about the tide, the shape of the waves, twilight and the changing of seasons. Starting again, I usually wake up at about 3 o'clock in the morning, head out around 3:30 and start shooting at 5 o'clock for the tide (at low tide, there are more stones in the foreground) and sunrise. In late winter and early spring, I rush to shoot green seaweeds, and in the hot summer, stones lay bare.

05   *Rational balance is composition*
         Color is impression
         Brushstrokes simple as intent
         Sea and mind at ease

Photography and painting have many similarities, but one ought to restart with a few prepared ideas! What kind of composition is required? What kind of brush strokes? What kind of color is there?

The quality of photographic composition provides mass, and my experience has given me a unique compositional style. Chinese compositional philosophy has developed earlier than the West: in Southern Song Dynasty, there was the compositional concept of "Ma [Yuan] on one corner, Xia [Gui] taking up half a side." Western compositional thinking emerged during the Renaissance, and rational thinking emphasized coherent, visual balance. I use photography as foundation and Renaissance rational balance as support, which forms my notion of composition.

Brush strokes are like signature, and the more personal aspects of painting. Oil painting addresses color blocks, and is what I need to learn the most. I studied Chinese *shanshui* landscape painting with Mr. Huang Chao-Hsiung for a period of time. Is it possible to replace color blocks with *cunfa* expressions of shade and texture? Should I relearn calligraphy and then practice *cunfa*? Thinking about it some more...I will do as I please! Who cares if the monk recites the scriptures properly? Romantic casualness is the conviction of my brushstroke.

How does one play with colors? This is another dilemma, maybe just paint! Crossing the river by feeling the stones, the boat will naturally straighten. After painting for about two months, one day I asked myself: what if I eliminate black like the Impressionists? Photography is without black, and I am fond of impressionistic tones, so I tried one painting, liked it, and bid adieu to black, and the tone was set.

06   *Painting from day to night,*
        like drum, like chime, beat into quiet
        Bach accompanies the brush
        Diligently advancing day by day, as waves chasing

For three years, I drew and painted five days a week from 8:00 to 18:00, like a recluse, rarely interacting with my former painter friends. In fact, many fellow students in Mr. Yim's studio encountered the same inquiry: do you leave? How do you find yourself? One day a fellow classmate came and visited me, noting the excellence of my stones by the sea, and asked me how I painted them. The next day I wrote a poem: "Portraits and stones are semblances. Semblances all lead to the way; if the way is obscure, then truth is unclear. When the way is clear, portraits and stones all point to truth." I was merely stating that Mr. Yim's forte in portraiture, his way of art through drawing portraits. If one sees merely portraits but not the way, then the way is blocked, but if one can see the path, then drawing stones or portraits are the same. I am only using Mr. Yim's methods of drawing portraits in painting stones.

Music is imperative when painting. Musical notes are like another invisible paintbrush, subtly affecting the shape and color of the painting. I love Beethoven, but painting with Beethoven doesn't always feel right, so I tried Brahms, which also didn't work...and Chopin, Mahler, Tchaikovsky, all don't work. Then I accidentally came across a Bach compilation of 144 CDs. I rarely listen to Bach, but for some reason I did not hesitate to buy it...and upon listening: Ah, it was perfect! Baroque music with its regularity and rhythm is very similar to waves, especially Bach's church cantatas. In his pious heart, there is a dialogue between man and God.

07   *A hundred miles of mist with a thousand days of painting*
        A thangka mandala in the first instance
        Mirroring the mind in the seascape and painting,
        there is no sea and no painting when the mind is true

One day, my interior designer friend Yawen came to visit me in my studio and said, "Simon! You are painting thangkas!" It seems appropriate when I think about it...When I was in Nepal and Tibet, seeing the master artists painting thangka: one stroke at a time; sometimes taking one year to complete one thangka. My process of painting is a bit like painting thangka. Coincidentally, two weeks after French pastel artist Sylvie Cabal came to my studio, she said, "You are drawing Mandala, and I am also drawing Mandala, just in different forms." She was formerly known for her floral paintings, a single flower composed on an entire sheet of paper, with segments of petals like geometric abstractions. She immediately showed me a photo of her new work, which has evolved into petals of mandala patterns, in soothing colors and style. She told me that she now feels surrounded by positive energy when she paints, no longer spent but very content. This is similar to my own feeling: I am no longer tired, but calm and at ease. Am I really painting thangka? Am I truly painting Mandala?

Thangka is a kind of portrait painted on cloth, silk, or paper in Tibet, covering a wide range of subjects, including the Buddha yidam, Dharma protectors and influential lamas, and matters of Tibetan life. Among them, the Mandala, also known as a "time-microcosm of the universe" is the most important, manifesting the Tibetan Buddhist view of the universe. It is the exploration of the mind through meditating on the Mandala, in reaching compatibility between the cosmos and man. For thousands of years, many Tibetan monks have created thangka paintings based on their inner mandala, in hopes of dialogue with the inner mandala of the viewer.

Everyone has their own mandala in their hearts. Some people have positive and clear mandalas, others negative and confused, but it is always the yardstick of our life values. When faced with a scene or an object, from sight to thought, thought to sense, sense to understanding, this is the dialogue between the authentic mandala and the inner mandala in our hearts. Likewise we will always be in conversation with past generations of this world, through the process of meditation-awakening-facing-reorganization-change. The practice and transformation of life is just between an instant.

After painting for another three years, my thoughts are like the sea, gradually changing into stones, persistent like stone, gradually transforming into the sea. The Sea Mandala is now clearer. Ah! It is time to share the Mandala with everyone.

The completion of a painting is the end of a fate and beginning of another. Now the paintings face not its creator, but more art lovers. Can the mandala of the painting speak to the mandala of the viewer? That is fate. Whether fate or not, is there Mandala? Is it Mandala? This is no longer important if it can bring a touch of dharma joy to the viewer, then that is enough!

As for why I paint? When I was a young man, I wanted to be a painter, but livelihood was the cause; with impromptu studies during middle age, expression was the cause; and now intensive practice, practice is the cause. All cause is interlocked and interconnected, and that may be our inescapable fate!

海的曼荼羅

海的曼荼羅

是　海　嗎？

聽　到　浪？

是　雲　嗎？

See the sea? Hear the waves? Is it a cloud?

Sea Mandala - Bf   80×130 cm / 60M / Oil on Canvas / 2017

Sea Mandala - Ac   80×116.5 cm / 50P / Oil on Canvas / 2016

Sea Mandala - Bh   89.5×130 cm / 60P / Oil on Canvas / 2017

Sea Mandala - Dh

100×250 cm / Oil on Canvas / 2019

Sea Mandala - Eb

120×240 cm / Oil on Canvas / 2020

Sea Mandala - Ae　　80×130 cm / 60M / Oil on Canvas / 2016

Sea Mandala - Bj   89.5×130 cm / 60P / Oil on Canvas / 2017

Sea Mandala - Ee

100×250 cm / Oil on Canvas / 2020

Sea Mandala - Ef

100×250 cm / Oil on Canvas / 2020

Sea Mandala - Ff

100×250 cm / Oil on Canvas / 2021

海 天 停 格？

四 季 不 動？

晨 光 永 在？

Sea and sky at a standstill?

Unwavering seasons?

Eternal morning light?

Sea Mandala - Bi   89.5×130 cm / 60P / Oil on Canvas / 2017

Sea Mandala - Ba　80×130 cm / 60M / Oil on Canvas / 2017

Sea Mandala - Ah   80×130 cm / 60M / Oil on Canvas / 2016

Sea Mandala - Dj

100×250 cm / Oil on Canvas / 2019

Sea Mandala - Ec

120×240 cm / Oil on Canvas / 2020

Sea Mandala - Ag   80×130 cm / 60M / Oil on Canvas / 2016

Sea Mandala - Bd　80×130 cm / 60M / Oil on Canvas / 2017

43

Sea Mandala - Eh

100×250 cm / Oil on Canvas / 2020

Sea Mandala - Dl
100×250 cm / Oil on Canvas / 2019

Sea Mandala - Fe

100×250 cm / Oil on Canvas / 2021

49

色 的 律 動？

筆 的 律 動？

相 的 律 動？

The cadence of color?

The cadence of the brush?

The cadence of Nimitta?

Sea Mandala - Ce   89.5×145.5 cm / 80M / Oil on Canvas / 2018

Sea Mandala - Ci   89.5×130 cm / 60P / Oil on Canvas / 2018

Sea Mandala - Aa   80×116.5 cm / 50P / Oil on Canvas / 2016

Sea Mandala - Ea

120×240 cm / Oil on Canvas / 2020

Sea Mandala - Df

110×220 cm / Oil on Canvas / 2019

Sea Mandala - Cf   89.5×130 cm / 60P / Oil on Canvas / 2018

Sea Mandala - Cb   89.5×145.5 cm / 80M / Oil on Canvas / 2018

Sea Mandala - De

110×220 cm / Oil on Canvas / 2019

Sea Mandala - Cj

89.5×179 cm / Oil on Canvas / 2018

Sea Mandala - Fh

100×250 cm / Oil on Canvas / 2021

浪　撲　石　？

碎　成　了　了　？

Waves against boulders?

Markedly shattered?

石　破　浪　？

如　如　不　動　？

Boulders breaking waves?

Equally unmoving?

Sea Mandala - Ai   80×130 cm / 60M / Oil on Canvas / 2016

Sea Mandala - Cg   89.5×130 cm / 60P / Oil on Canvas / 2018

Sea Mandala - Bk   89.5×130 cm / 60P / Oil on Canvas / 2017

Sea Mandala - Eg

100×250 cm / Oil on Canvas / 2020

Sea Mandala - Ck

89.5×179 cm / Oil on Canvas / 2018

Sea Mandala - Ch   89.5×130 cm / 60P / Oil on Canvas / 2018

Sea Mandala - Bg   89.5×130 cm / 60P / Oil on Canvas / 2017

Sea Mandala - Di

100×250 cm / Oil on Canvas / 2019

Sea Mandala - Dk

100×250 cm / Oil on Canvas / 2019

Sea Mandala - Fg

100×250 cm / Oil on Canvas / 2021

海 畫 是 假？

畫 海 是 真？

Is my sea painting an imitation?

Am I truly painting the sea?

Am I truly painting the sea?

Is my sea painting an imitation?

海 畫 是 假？

畫 海 是 真？

Sea Mandala - Ab   80×116.5 cm / 50P / Oil on Canvas / 2016

Sea Mandala - Bb　　80×130 cm / 60M / Oil on Canvas / 2017

Sea Mandala - Bc   80×130 cm / 60M / Oil on Canvas / 2017

Sea Mandala - Dc

110×220 cm / Oil on Canvas / 2019

Sea Mandala - Ed

120×240 cm / Oil on Canvas / 2020

Sea Mandala - Be   80×130 cm / 60M / Oil on Canvas / 2017

Sea Mandala - Ca   89.5×145.5 cm / 80M / Oil on Canvas / 2018

Sea Mandala - Dd

110×220 cm / Oil on Canvas / 2019

Sea Mandala - Fc
90×270 cm
Oil on Canvas / 2021

Sea Mandala - Fd

90×270 cm

Oil on Canvas / 2021

我　畫　海？　　　　海　畫　我？

畫　成　海　的　曼　荼　羅

I paint the sea?

The sea paints me?

Painting into Sea Mandala.

Sea Mandala - Cd   89.5×145.5 cm / 80M / Oil on Canvas / 2018

Sea Mandala - Bl　89.5×130 cm / 60P / Oil on Canvas / 2017

Sea Mandala - Af   80×130 cm / 60M / Oil on Canvas / 2016

Sea Mandala - Dg

100×250 cm / Oil on Canvas / 2019

Sea Mandala - Fi

110×220 cm / Oil on Canvas / 2021

Sea Mandala - Fj

110×220 cm / Oil on Canvas / 2021

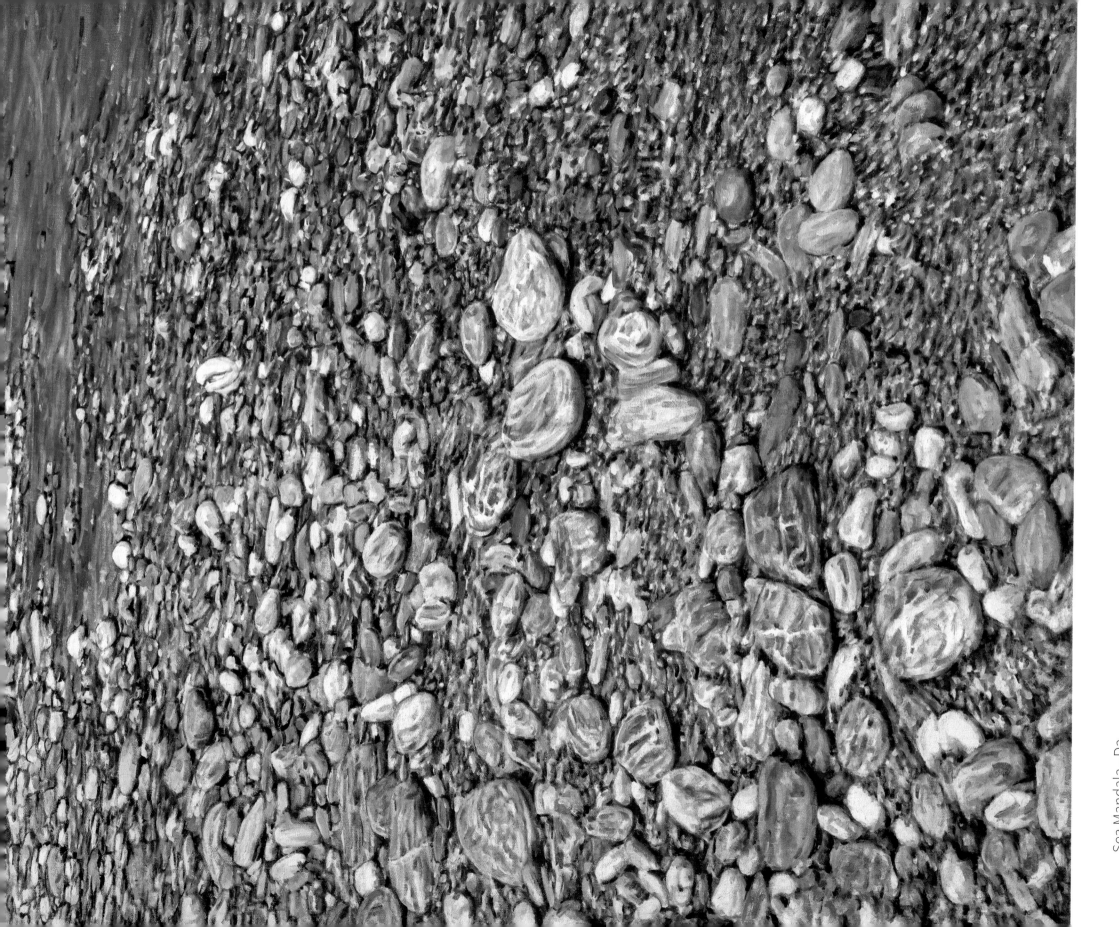

Sea Mandala - Da
220×110 cm / Oil on Canvas / 2019

Sea Mandala - Fb

200×120 cm / Oil on Canvas / 2021

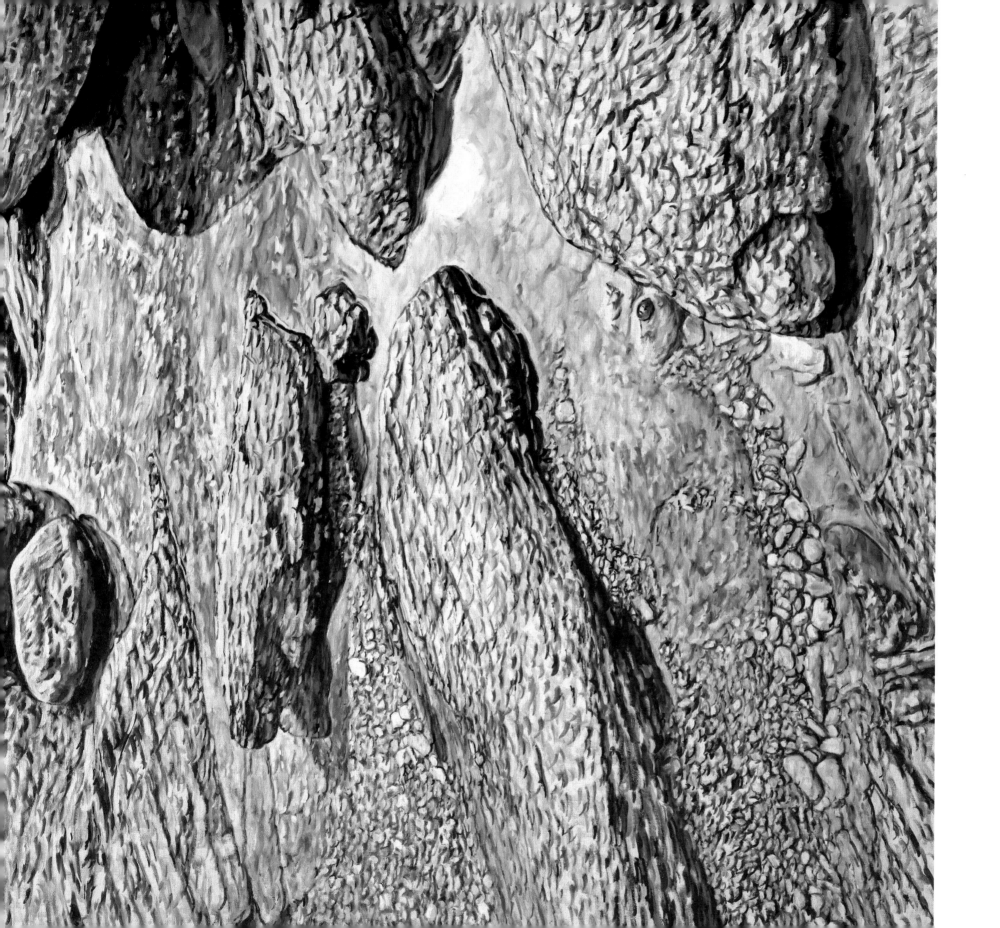

Sea Mandala - Fa

200×120 cm / Oil on Canvas / 2021

See/Sea Mandala.

Sea Mandala - Ad   80×116.5 cm / 50P / Oil on Canvas / 2016

海的曼荼羅

海的曼荼羅

See/Sea Mandala

書　名：海的曼荼羅
作　者：王慎敏
發行人：吳　放
封面題字：黃守正
策展人：王暉之

總編輯：王暉之
展覽總監：陳耀姬
美術設計：林恬慈
美術編輯：黃靖閔
英文翻譯：朱雨平
影音製作：吳杭之
行銷企劃：吳采頻
印刷製作：威創彩藝

出版發行：長歌藝術傳播有限公司
發行地址：105 台北市松山區南京東路 4 段 106 號 3 樓
展覽地址：114 台北市內湖區堤頂大道二段 407 巷 32 號 1 樓
電　話：+886-2-33223338
網　站：長歌藝術傳播 www.veryartist.com.tw
郵政劃撥：50270987
帳　戶：長歌藝術傳播有限公司

初版日期：2021 年 6 月
ＩＳＢＮ：978-986-99298-4-4
定　價：NT$ 1200 元

Title: See/Sea Mandala
Author: Simon Wang
Publisher: Wu Fund
Calligraphy: Shou-Chen Huang
Curator: Aurore Wang

Chief Editor: Aurore Wang
Executive Art Director: Claire Chen
Art Designer: Tien-Tzu Lin
Layout: Jamie Huang
English Translation: Daphne Chu
Videography: James Wu
Marketing: Tammy Wu
Printed and bound in Taiwan by We-Create-We-Print Printing Co. Ltd.

Publishing House : Chang Ge Arts & Media Ltd.
Address: 3F., No.106, Sec. 4, Nanjing E. Rd., Songshan Dist., Taipei City 105, Taiwan (R.O.C.)
Exhibition Venue: 1F., No.32, Ln. 407, Sec. 2, Tiding Blvd., Neihu Dist., Taipei City 114, Taiwan (R.O.C.)
Telephone: +886-2-33223338
Website: www.veryartist.com.tw
Postal Transfer: 50270987
Account: Chang Ge Arts & Media Ltd.

First Print: June 2021
I S B N: 978-986-99298-4-4
Price: NT$ 1200